LOVE:

Poems by
Danielle Steel

A Dell Book

Published by
Dell Publishing
a division of
Bantam Doubleday Dell Publishing Group, Inc.
1540 Broadway
New York, New York 10036

The cover format and design of this book are protected trade dresses and trademarks of Dell Publishing, a division of Bantam Doubleday Dell Publishing Group, Inc.

Some of the poems in this book first appeared in *Cosmopolitan, The Paraclete, McCalls, Ladies' Home Journal,* and *Good Housekeeping.*

The trademark Dell® is registered in the U.S. Patent and Trademark Office.

ISBN: 0-440-15377-8

Printed in the United States of America

Designed by Giorgetta Bell McRee

One Previous Dell Edition

New Dell Edition

August 1989

30 29 28

OPM

To John, with all my love,
d.s.

Contents

1

When Love Is New

—First Meeting—

Razzle
  dazzle
    snow scene,
my life
  so white
    so bare
      so vast,
and then
  your open
    door,
my heart
  whooshing
    toward
your arms,
  racing
    much
      too fast,
too free,
  as your eyes
waltzed
  slowly
    over me,

the cadence
yours,
the tempo
mine,
the music
poured
like
vintage
wine,
the magic
of our moment
so rare,
so good,
so new,
as breathlessly,
I gazed
at you.

Fragments
of two
lives
sifted
through
fine wire,
spread out
like
fans,
added
and
subtracted
and shaken up
like dice,
then rolled
across
a board,
a map,
your life
laid
gently
out

before
me,
mine
tossed
helter
skelter
in your
lap.

Waiting for Your Call

Backing
  and sidling
hurting
  ribs
    within
      my stall,
fighting,
  fleeing,
    running,
      seeing,
hoping,
  dying,
    aching,
      being,
waiting
  for
the soft
  ring
    of your
      call.

Poem to *Danny*

It doesn't matter
   at all
      if you
         call,
if you care,
   if you dare,
if you
   dream,
if
   you sing
      in a tree.
It doesn't matter
   at all,
      not at all
         ...just
            to me.

Shuffled Papers

Clumsily,
  but gently,
I push
  you
    from
      my head,
as I fumble
  at my desk,
shuffle
  papers,
try to see
  and think
    and do,
when all
  I find
    beneath
      my hand,
        my eye,
my heart,
  is
    you.

Comfortable
   in my ivory tower,
barren,
   lonely,
      safe,
hidden,
   shrunken,
      tiny,
         small,
and then you,
   suddenly
      peeking
         over my wall,
with firelit eyes
   and dazzling smile,
I flew away,
   I ran a mile,
I hid from you,
   I shoved you back,
      and then you called,
I felt
   my lack,
      my ache,

your eyes,
    your smile,
I turned again,
   I ran a mile,
feeling all
   your charms,
hungering
  for your arms,
wondering if
   I'd come
     to harm
or safe,
   listening for
     your voice...
knowing that I had
  no choice.

El Señor

You take a matador stance,
   I see you do it,
standing very near,
   you let me brush by,
tucking in your soul,
   looking very whole
     and strong and free,
yet never touching,
   reaching out to me,
    but always there,
you carry fire and smiles
   like darts and banners,
your manner
   pulls me closer,
    I brush near once again,
rushing through your cape,
   you smile,
    you watch,
     you know,
      you wait,
and I fly on and on
   again,
    ever closer,

ever faster,
ever more,
and ever farther
from the safety
of the gate.

Your Call

I wait now
   every morning,
      every day,
         for your voice,
your call,
   your smile,
      your hand,
         your eyes...
waiting for the phone
   to ring,
I realize
   how hard
      I hope
for a reason,
   an excuse,
      a word,
         a game,
an anything,
   a joke,
      a song,
         a ring...
I wait
   and then

I hear
your voice
at last...
I smile...
I fly,
I sing!

Party Shoes

Brown galoshes
  and red party shoes,
    my old life
      and my new,
my days alone,
  my life with you,
    funny funky
      old galoshes,
sad and brown and cold,
  then you, my love,
    smiling, sparkling,
      shy yet bold,
changing my life,
  my world,
    my blues,
to dazzling,
  dancing,
    party shoes

—Zippety Click—
I Love You

Zippety click,
   hop and skip
      from one thing
        to another,
dancing,
   running,
having one sweet
   hell of a good
      time,
zippety click,
   involvement
all those
   lovely causes
      to espouse,
and people
   to be met,
until quite
   suddenly
      today,

everything
    went Pow!
I love you,
    can you even
      start
        to think
of such a silly
    joke
      today?
I love you,
    by golly,
      yes,
        I do.
I do love you
    today.

From Opposite Ends

From opposite ends
  of the earth
    we came,
trundling
  our bags,
    our treasures,
our laughter,
  our
    hearts.
From opposite ends
  of the city
    we came,
from different points
  where we
    once stood,
so near,
  yet far apart.
From opposite ends
  of the world
    we came,

silent and cautious,
   unseen.
From opposite ends
   of a lifetime
      we came,
and found
   a breath
      of magic
         hovering
            in between.
From opposite ends
   of a kiss
      we come,
to hold
   each other
      tight
         beneath
            a starry sky.
From opposite ends
   of a heart
      we smile,
two lives
   blended
      into one,
with no more
   opposites
      to approach,

but simply together,
   laughing
      and young,
the beautiful man
   that you are,
      and I.

Each of Us

Each of us
   with our
      secret gifts,
magic potions,
   lovely notions,
      waiting to be
       shared,
waiting to be
   aired,
each of us
   a half,
a whole,
   a mind,
      a soul,
       a heart,
and yet
   a part
of a better
   richer
      more,
       looking for the
door,
   the key,

the you,
the me,
the we
growing
day by day,
looking
for the way
to find
what
I'd always
dreamed
and never seen,
always tried
and never been,
always thought
but never knew,
until at last
I discovered
that the gift
I always sought
was you.

The rest
  of the world
    sits
      around
        in a knot,
a complicated
  ball
    of strangled
      confusion
and bungled
  hopes
    beyond
      repair.
While we
  in simple
    silence
have our
  private
    miracle
      to share.
O pity
  the poor
    tangled,

strangled
knots,
which we,
thank God,
are
not!

Are You Comfortable?

Are you
  comfortable?
Can you
  breathe?
Two pillows
  or one?
Is my arm
  crushing
    yours?
Is your
  leg
    wedged
      too tight
        under mine?
Are my hipbones
  too pointy?
    My nipples
      too
        small?
Oh, stranger

asleep
at my side
here
tonight,
are you
warm?
Am I
safe?
Could you
love me
at all?

Daughter of
Love

I've never laughed
 when I made
  love
   before,
never touched
 tenderly
  and kissed,
feeling
 young
  and old,
and then
 rolled
  over
   slowly
with a smile
 of glee,
as looking up,
 you kiss
  my eyes,
and say

something
silly,
teasing
me.
I never knew
that a bed
was
a place,
where
people
shared
their hearts
with smiles.
I never
made love
with
a giggle
before,
laughing
and glowing,
and silently
knowing
that
laughter
is part
of the art,

like hands
   are to gloves....
I just never knew
   that laughter
      was sweet
and so much
   a daughter
      of love.

Jam

Jam.
    There must be jam,
        you told me
            firmly,
with a half-hidden
    smile
        of satisfaction
and a promise
    I was yet
        to understand.
You were making
    your presence known.
Toast.
    Eggs perhaps.
        Double coffee,
            some milk,
                one sugar,
maybe juice,
    but always,
        always
            jam.
Yes, I understand.
    I think I can

manage
that,
monsieur,
even in my halfstate
in the morning
And you sat
watching
with the smile
that made me feel,
so bright, so gay,
so light...
and then I knew
you'd spend
the night....
You did, my love,
and there was
breakfast
in the morning,
with birds
singing,
hearts flying,
sun streaming
in over scrambled eggs,
and ham...
and, oh, yes,
of course...
there was jam.

—*Nary a Care*—

You're gone,
   new lover.
Gone
   to your day,
      to your life,
         to your way
            of doing things,
whatever it is
   you do,
      when you are far
         from me.
And I,
   like a child
      with a dream,
gaze
   starry-eyed
      into the summer
         rain,
feeling anguish,
   gentle
      pain,
fearing
   you will vanish

from the bright
universe
we created
side by side
last night.
And then,
in bittersweet
despair,
I linger
with a cup of tea,
fearing
you have forgotten me,
feeling foolish,
old with fright,
yet young
with promise
long forgotten
in my distant
dreams....
And suddenly,
you're at
the door,
full of brand-new
schemes
for this path
we choose
to share.

Home from your wars,
from your tasks,
from your day,
with nary a care
and only more love
to strew
on my way.
I rush
to your arms
with a gurgle
of laughter,
a thunder
of glee.
Dream man
come true,
you actually
did
come back
to me!

Moonlit Sunshine

What
  do you
    do
for me
  with me
    to me?
You
  send
    silver
      sparkle
thunder
  moonlit
    sunshine
      shivers
through
  and through
    and through
      me.

2

Growing Together

Sunshine Dancing

Heavenly, heavenly
   mornings
      unraveling
         our bodies
and then tying them
   in a fresh knot
      with sleepy smiles
         and tender words,
as morning birds
   sing past our window,
      sunshine dancing
         on our life,
and I for the first time
   ever
      feeling like
         a wife,
yet lover, friend,
   making breakfast,
      smiling to myself
as I burn the toast,
   and break the eggs,

still feeling
   your hands
      and kisses
         on my legs...
surely this is what
   life
      always had in store...
oh, darling,
   you make me ache for you,
      always hungry,
         always glad,
            always wanting more...

Ordinary
Pleasures

I love our mornings,
  waking,
    finding you there
      next to me,
    smiling,
desperately needing
  that first cigarette
    to start your day,
and then dashing off
  to make you eggs,
seeing visions of
  your face,
    your hands,
      your legs,
your back
  as I juggle coffee,
    butter toast,
and wonder what
  I love the most
    about all that it is
      you are,

brightest star
    in my heavens,
        answer to all my
            unborn dreams
                and secret wishes,
I clatter dishes and
    arrive
        to help you undress
            after you have just put
                yourself together,
the weather is sublime
    and we are fine,
and you are more precious
    than you know,
        as we both begin to
            glow,
it is another perfect day...
    and then you're on your way
        to work
            and I, wife-style,
                driving,
thriving on the rich
    delights
        we share,
the tiny ordinary pleasures,
    I come home

and tuck into my heart
like wondrous
sparkling
tiny treasures.

Friend

My house
  my car
    my bed
      my arms
my life
  my soul
    my smiles
      and all
        my dreams
are touched
  by the magic
    of your
      sounds,
your
  smell,
the perfume
  of your life
intertwined
  with mine
    in a silvery
      blend,
so that I can

think
of only
you,
precious
lover,
partner,
friend.

──── *Comfortable* ────

You shout at me
and I yell
back,
you push,
I shove,
and we squabble
comfortably
over who sleeps
where,
which side,
whose spot,
you are,
I'm not,
you won't,
I will,
you grouse,
I'm shrill,
a symphony
of loving,
a song
for every day,
a way

to say
"I love you"
in our own
   familiar way.

Bill

I love your macho swagger,
   the look in your eye,
    in your smile,
    all the while
      you move toward me.
You always seem to know
  I'm there,
sometimes I sit back
  and stare
   quietly
    for a while,
waiting for you to know
  I'm near.
You sense it,
  see me,
and walk purposefully
  toward where I wait,
as I fall in love
  with you again,
watching your special
  just you
   macho
    gait.

Rainbow Dreams

As evening comes,
   I race,
already hungry
   for your face,
      your hand,
         your touch,
so much you have
   to give,
      and lavish on me
         with such style...
I think of you...
   I see you smile...
my heart dances,
   prances,
      runs, cavorts,
         and preens,
as quickly
   I do my face,
      my hair,
         and wait for you,
            with a myriad
of rainbow dreams.

Ball of Yarn

I have this funny
   ball of yarn
     in the corner
       of my head.
It sits there
   nice and neat
     and then I walk over,
       pick it up,
         look at it,
smile,
   and then I start
     to worry it
       a little,
just because it's
   there,
and then it starts
   to look all
     tangled up
       and messy
and I start
   to trip
     and fall
       in my ball of yarn.

Then you come home
  and gently
    pluck it
      from my hands,
smooth it out
  and make it
    neat
      again,
set it down,
  and smile at it
    with me
and I know
  again
    why I'm so glad
      when you come home.

Zigzag

Dashing
zigzag
across
the pattern
of our life,
playing
husband,
mother,
genius,
wife,
scholar,
chauffeur,
student,
friend,
then finding
you alone,
for a fraction
of a moment,
a sliver
of a day,
loving
what you are

and wish
   and try to be
in a very
   very
      special
      way.

— Love's Tango —

In an anthill,
  in a tree,
    in a crowd
      of sixty-three,
I feel
  lost
    and then
      confused,
but smile
  at you,
    bemused,
you squeeze
  my hand,
    we swim
      for land,
you hold
  my arm
and render
  harm
    a useless thing,
      a broken
        spear.

With you,
my love,
I know
no fear.
Only
warmth
and sunny skies
that dance
love's
tango
in
your eyes.

Okay,
    okay
        so
            I'll be
                cool.
At least
    I can
        pretend
            to be,
since
    you can't
        see
            me
near
    the phone,
        or lying
            in the bath
                at night,
wondering
    if
        you'll
            marry
                me.

3

Growing Apart

Peeling
Away

I feel you
   peeling
away
   from
     me,
like sticking
   plaster
     tearing
       slowly
from a wound,
  a layer
of my skin
   soldered
     to yours
       until
suddenly
   slowly
infinitely
   painfully,
you began

to pull,
just
    a little
        not
            a lot,
just enough
    to make me
        wonder,
and then
    suddenly
all of it
    being torn
        asunder,
my heart
    with its
        top
            popped,
drunk
    emptied,
        finished,
            gone,
                and now the

rest
    of me
        pried
            loose,
                torn free,

and I tired,
      frightened,
         crying,
             wondering
                 why
you can't
     love
          me.

Recapture
the Dream

I want to come back
   to you,
want to feel happy
   about you again,
I want to look up
   at your eyes
      and giggle with glee,
not see
   the reflection
      of the pain you've caused me.
I want to feel merry
   and good,
and grateful for your love,
   not distant and remote
      and somewhere
         far
            above.
I want to fly
   to your arms
      like a child

sailing
off
a swing.
I want to remember
the warmth
your loving can bring.
I'm so tired
of the chill,
the winter,
the snow.
Can't we rekindle
the fires,
and bring back the glow?
So much between us,
So much sorrow
it would seem...
oh, distant man,
help me
recapture
the dream.

Trying to Pretend

Trying
  to pretend
    I'm cool,
lying
  in the bed
that is
  absolutely
    vast
      without you.
Trying to pretend
  that I
    don't
      care
how late
  your key
    plays
      chimes
        in my ear
as it turns
  in the lock.

Trying to pretend
 I'm
   free
but stayed
  home
    only
      because
        it rained
and I
  was tired
    tonight.
Trying to pretend
  that I
    don't
      care
but caring
  far
    too
      much.
Trying to pretend
  that I don't
    give
      a damn
        about you,
my one
  and only
    man.

So go out.
   Go ahead.
Don't come home.
   Stay out.
      Get drunk.
         Get laid.
            Fly free.
I'll be here
   all night tonight,
trying to pretend
   I am
      the super splendid
         lady cool
I can't
   even
      begin
         to pretend
            to be.

Regret

Someday I will learn,
   I will stand stately,
      proud,
         noble, dear,
            as you expect.
And reluctantly
   relinquish
      the unpredictable,
uncontrollable child
   you have known.
That look of dark despair,
   of fear,
suspicion,
   of "oh...what now?"
      that you glaze me with
      in darker hours.
Fierce frown,
   flashing eyes,
brows so tightly knit,
   they bristle
      to discourage
         girlish prattle,

that prattle is the last shout
    of those baby days
        you long to know.
Sometimes mere girlish glee,
    harmless,
        yet unwanted.
Someday it will fade
    slowly, unnoticed.
Till it is gone,
    and I will have become
        the woman,
            and not the girl.
The girl will vanish
    if you wish it so.
Will you be proud?
    I don't believe you will.
Too late, my love,
    too late,
        and we shall share
            Regret.

You run
   in and out
      of my simple
         life,
as though
   it were
      a game,
a child's sport,
   a sort of
      forest
where you can
   dart
      among
         the trees.
Now I see
   you,
      now I
         don't.
Perhaps you
   will,
      perhaps
         you won't.

The phone lies
    still.
It means
    you're happy
        somewhere
        else.
The phone
    then comes
        alive again.
It means
    you're tired
        of the world
        of men.
You come,
    you go,
        you flit,
            you fly,
You run into
    my arms,
you lie.
    You disappear.
And then I see
    you,
        standing there,
playing
    peekaboo

behind
a tree.
Oh, no.
No more.
This time
I score.
Farewell,
poor childish man.
Have your fun.
Live your life.
Play all your games.
But not
with me.

Where do you go
  when you go out
    for milk
      and come back
        seven hours later?
What happens
  when you park
    the car
      and go home
        somewhere else?
Whose cigarettes
  are you buying
    when you go out
      for mine
and come back
  with the wrong brand?
Whose name do you
  mutter
    in your sleep?
What heart do you
  keep
    in your pocket,
      hidden from my eyes?

What lies will you
   concoct next,
    my dear,
while I pretend
   that I don't fear
    the end
which came so long ago
   while I pretended
    not to hear
its deathlike
   footstep
    on my heart?

Motorcycle,
   airplane
      noises,
hot rock
   on the stereo
      in your car,
swift step
   and static
      always
         in the air.
Ever quicker
   pace
      hastening
         away
from peace
   toward
      noise,
playing
   volleyball
      amidst
         the people
            in your life.

Run faster
    faster
        still
midst
    your self-created
        noise
that will never
    kill
        the angry
            whispers
                of your soul.

A thousand dreams
  we shared,
    a thousand tears
     we shed,
a thousand days,
  a thousand nights,
    a thousand joys,
      a thousand fights,
a thousand episodes,
  a thousand epithets,
    a thousand hopes
    you shattered
      at my feet,
a thousand hearts
  you scattered
    and then mine,
and all the time
  I thought
    you cared,
how rare
  the joke,
    how sweet the gag,

how much I thought
  you loved
    this hag
a thousand years
  ago,
    my dear,
a thousand moments
  strung like tears,
    icicles across
      my soul,
a thousand ways
  of letting love,
    once oh so warm,
      die softly,
and then grow
  very
    very
      cold.

Only violets,
   I only wanted
      violets,
not masses of
   red roses,
      and vulgar ribbons,
         and finery,
            and lies.
I only wanted
   violets,
just two
   or three,
      or scribbles
         in the sand,
a trinket,
   some small
      thought,
a warm hand
   in the rain,
a smile,
   an apple,
      or some trifling

imperfection
  I could love.
Too much,
  and much too little.
A turtle,
  yes, a turtle
    would be nice too,
three-leaf clovers
  and fading leaves,
not stifling vulgarity
  and expensive emptiness.
But now I know how
  costly are the trifles,
how dear
  and almost
    unattainable.
Just violets,
  my love,
just that,
  remember it
    next year.

Carved in *Stone*

You carve me
  in stone now
with your
  lazy
    finger
      sculpting
       me,
etching
  the icy
    nooks
you once made
  soft
    and warm,
you carve me
  in stone
    now
with the plastic
  passion
    of your
      torch,

shooting
  tinfoil
    sparks
        at my flinching
            marble.
You carved me
  differently
    before,
turned
  my wood
    to bark,
        bearing leaves,
giving birth
  to flowers
with the powers
  of your
    burning
      love,
which secretly,
  we both know
    burns
      no
        more,
as your lukewarm,
  too weak,
    too quick
      to chill,

fraying magic
    forces me
        to speak,
when once
    silence
        was
            enough.
Now,
    after you are
        rough,
you ask
    "happy?"
        just before
            you go,
and silently
    I nod
        my head,
whispering
    softly
        "no."

I dread you
   now,
dread
   your touch
and the smile
   that doesn't
     warm
      me
       anymore.
I dread you
   now,
your hand
   that frightens,
     makes me
      flinch
and hurts me
   to
     the
      core.
I dread
   you
     now,

your anger
quicker
than
the laughter
that
we
knew.
I dread you
now,
dread
the sight
of all
that
I
no longer
see
in
you.

Nothingness

A man
  touched me
    today,
and covered me
  with
    nothing,
a man
  I used to
    love,
the one
  I cared
    about
      so much,
but this time
  as he
    touched me
      with his nothingness,
there was only
  shock
    to realize
how far
  behind
    I'd left
      him.

The Year of the Bears

Side by side
  through the winter,
    tucked in
      like bears,
we snuggled
  and hugged
    and shared
      all our cares,
we teased
  and we talked,
and we whispered
  a lot,
until suddenly
  spring
    and at once
      you were
        not...
not mine
  and not there,
not here
  and nowhere,

your eyes
empty
in mine,
your lies
never
on time,
until finally,
grieving,
I knew
from your trend,
that our
magical,
mystical,
marvelous
year of the bears
had come
to
an
end.

Desperation

In desperation
　I counted
　　on my fingers
　　　whom to call,
to turn to,
　reach out for,
　　cling to.
Seven, eight,
　nine
　　people
　　　to hold
　　　　close...
nine,
　seven,
　　four,
　　　none.
Mistaken
　I had been
　　in desperation,

finding that
　　others wouldn't
　　　　do.
I only
　　wanted
　　　him.

I Go

I can't bear it
  anymore,
    I can't...
too much anger,
  too much pain,
    too much sorrow,
      too much rain,
no matter how madly
  we once
    loved
      each other,
I can't trudge
  another
    step
on this lonely
  journey
    by myself...
left here
  on the shelf
where you put me
  for safekeeping,
I sit here,
  always weeping,
    waiting

for your return,
while deep inside
  I burn
    with slow despair...
I care...
  oh, darling,
    yes, I care...
but now I can't,
  I won't,
I will not sit here
  dying,
    fading,
      crying,
loving,
  hating,
    waiting
      for the fates
to deposit you
  in my arms
    once more
with your smile
  so rich and slow...
oh, no, my love,
  I can't
    love you or not,
      this time...
        I go.

Silence on the Stair

I watch
  the top
    of his head
as he travels
  quickly
    downward
into the vortex
  of the spiral
    staircase,
running
  down,
lightly
  like water
    down a mountainside,
his feet
  barely touching
    one step
before they rush
  headlong
    toward
      another...

he waves
   his hand,
      then looks
         up,
sunlight
   dancing
      on his face.
It is
   a moment
      filled
         with grace...
and then
   despair.
Before
   I gave
      my heart
         its head
to tell
   its tale,
I let him
   go,
I let him
   flee,
to dance
   his freedom
      dance
         so far from me.

Gone now.
Gone.
And only
silence
on the
stair.

4

Letting Go

Free

Setting the bird free,
  raven haired,
    soaring high above my head,
watching him,
  wings stretched out,
with only a brief last look
  back,
circling high,
  wider now,
pride swooping low
  in my heart,
and coursing through
  my veins,
pride
  because I set him
    free,
only to remember
  all too quickly
    that it was not
      I,
    but he,
and with a last tender
  look

at my now empty
    horizon,
I know that he was
    always
      free.
Gone now,
   raven bird,
      gone to your own sun,
far from mine,
    far from here now,
much beloved bird,
    fly well,
      soar high,
        go free.

What is it like for you right now?
   Is the snow as grayish
     as the world you left behind?
Is it all as filled
   with being busy,
is it as much effort
   to laugh harder than the crowd?
Have you told as many
   funny stories?
Have you almost cried
   as many times?
Or are you really having fun,
   the very best of times,
and feeling much relieved
   to be cavorting
     in the snow,
and very far away at last,
   feeling that you have
     escaped
before the time could come
   when people don't turn back?
Or worse,

have you just forgotten
        everything that passed?
Are you being happy?
    Or feeling quite bereft
        the way I do?

Crash into
My Life

Did you mean
  to crash
    into my life
      this way,
leaving everything
  so topsy-turvy
    as you left?
Do you mean
  to tell me
    that you
      didn't know
        I'd care?
Did you really
  think I'd laugh
    and walk
      away?
How small you must have
  thought me,
if even
  for a moment
    you believed

I could
smell roses
in the air
and taste
champagne
again,
and walk
away
at midnight
to rake
my leaves
and give up
life again.

If I Can

How do I find my way back
  from the place
    where you
      led me?
The arbor,
  the swing,
    the lilac,
      the ring,
the promises, the dawn,
  the dreams
    that they spawned.
I understand.
  It is all different now,
    you aren't a boy,
      you're a man.
But show me, my love,
  the way back
    from it all,
and I'll follow the path
  if I can.

Sketch

That sketch of you
   so perfect
     at the time,
so endearing
   because you smiled
     above it
as we stared at it
   together,
     pleased.
Now it stares
   at me,
     alone,
and hangs coldly
   on my wall,
no longer part
   of you,
     or us,
no longer anyone
   I even
     once
       remotely knew.

It is but
      a strong man s
         face,
your kind
   of eyes.
A man
   in a beret.
Someone
   born here
      on my wall.
It could be
   anyone
      but you,
in fact
   it is
      no one
         at all.

Fingering Our Sand

Going back
    to tender places,
        full of you,
touching
    once warm
        moments,
            looking at
our sun,
    standing
        twixt
            our sea
                and sky,
and fingering
    our sand,
        looking at
            the places
we both
    once wore
        like hats,

I wondered where
the moments
went,
flying past
my head
like cranes
and darting
through
my feet
like rats.

Silence

Your silence hurts,
　　it weighs heavily,
　　　　dammit,
I cared so bloody much,
　　I hurt, I gave,
　　　　I cried,
　　　　　　I wanted,
needed,
　　hoped,
　　　　the scope
　　　　　　of it all
　　　　　　　　still overwhelms me
as I paint portraits
　　in the sky,
　　　　seeing you
　　　　　　in my life's eye,
　　　　　　　　painting in
your presence
　　for a thousand years
　　　　to come,
wanting, wishing,
　　hoping,
　　　　seeing,

yet frightened
   that
      you'll
         fade away...
and then,
   trembling,
      I realize
         once more...
there was no call
   from you
      today.

No One There

I offer him
   silence
     and take back
       despair.
I look
   for a rainbow
     and find
       only dust.
I wish
   for a dream
     and wake up
       in a trance.
I cling
   to a smile
     and choke
       on a sob.
I tender
   my hand
     and bring back
       the air.

I reach
for the man
and find
no one
there.

Soaring
Silver Bird

Soaring silver bird
  in the noonday
    sky,
weighted
  with the man
    who chose
      to leave me.
I wish
  for safety,
pray
  for flame,
knowing hotly,
  in the midst
    of my confusion
      that
        flame
or no
  he will be
    dead
      to me
        now.

Fear Not — Farewell

Fear not,
　　sweet love,
the hands
　　of time,
for poems
　　do not
　　　always
　　　　rhyme,
fate runs
　　its course
　　　and plays
　　　　its tricks
and in the
　　last
　　　and final
　　　　mix,
one wins
　　it
　　　all
　　　　and loses
　　　　　naught,

if love
   was good
      and battles
         fought
to their
   very
      final
         end,
good-bye,
   sweet love,
farewell,
   my friend.

Fragile Moments

Shock.
Blast.
Zap.
Gone.
Gone?
Gone.
He's gone
now.
Dead.
Finished.
Over.
Yes,
gone.
And strange
how it
all works,
how it
happens,
what lasts
in one's
mind.

Only the
    tiny
        fragile
            moments,
                the unlikely
gems,
    the morsels,
        and not
            the cake,
the taste
    of the whole
        forgotten,
and only
    the faint
        perfume
            of unreality
                remains...
his whims...
    his smile,
        the guileless
            way he looked
only once
    or twice,
        and in a thrice
            he's gone,

the tale
     too brief
       to tell,
and you remember
     nothing
        very long
          or
             very well.

5

Lonely Feelings

Couples.
  Happy couples,
clinging close,
  hugging tight,
    dancing fast,
      being one,
laughing loud,
  singing high,
    giggling shrill,
      showing off,
loving love,
  living hard,
    and making
      my heart
break
  and
    snap
      and
die
  as
    I
      watch
        them

from
this
spot
where
I
still
stand
alone.

Two Thirds

Two thirds
    and two thirds.
Two apartments,
    two separate
        homes,
            neighbors.
Together
    we make
        four thirds,
one
    too
        much
and twice
    one
        short.
You have
    your
        man,
            neighbor woman,
and I
    my child,
and as your husband

trotted
down
the
stairs
today
with his dog
and my child,
I watched
his legs,
the sway
of his hips,
the way
his haircut
ended,
and you watched
my small girl's
bright red
sneakers,
starlit hair
and tiny hand
clasped
in his
larger
one.

Two thirds
we are
in either
house,
and neither
of us
whole.

Woman
Laughing
in the Night

Shrilly,
  a voice
    in the night
caw caws
  raven-fashion,
it is a cactus
  sound,
it prickles me,
  and, curious,
    I rise,
stealthily
  pulling back
    lace curtains
that have
  come to me
    too soon.
Silently
  I watch...

a taxi
     giving birth
          to a man,
               and then
                    a woman.
She laughs again.
     She gropes
          for him,
throwing back
     her head,
hurling
     laughter
          from her mouth
again
     like sparks
          this time,
               staccato,
                    sharp,
he fondles her,
     the cab leaves,
          I watch.
She laughs again
     and he silences
          her,
               but only for an instant,
               with a kiss.

She laughs
    she holds his hand
        she leads him
            home,
her prey
    into her laughter lair.
while I,
    too soon old
        while still
            so young,
watch,
    bereft,
        alone,
            unseen.

On the Riverbank

Two men once
   found
     me
naked
   on the riverbank
     at different
       times,
and then
   a third
     came by.
All brothers,
   all the same,
     seeking
only
   naked
     maidens
near a
   body
     of cool
       water

to quench
　their many
　　thirsts.
Two men
　left me
　　on that
　　　riverbank,
the third
　left
　　me
　　　for dead,
and if
　a fourth
　　should
　　　happen
　　　　by,
he'll not
　find me
　　on the
　　　riverbank
listening
　for his
　　tread.
He'll find
　me
　　armed
　　　and shielded,

hidden
near
a strong,
stone wall,
if a fourth
should even
happen
to find me
there
at all.

Boat Come In, Tide Go Out

I sat and watched
   a boat
      come in,
the tide
   go out,
a bird
   fly by,
a man
   swim past,
a life
   go by.
The sun
   had set,
the man
   had gone,
the tide
   was out,

the day
   was done,
the life
   gone by
was mine.

Princes,
　　toads,
　　　　and butterflies,
sugar cookies,
　　bitter apple tarts,
　　　　and frosty lemonades,
circus tents,
　　and puppy dogs,
　　　　and hayrides,
icy midnight
　　swimming
　　　　in a lake,
muddy roads,
　　woodsy smells,
　　　　fresh grass,
and dandelions,
　　and oranges,
　　　　and wine,
faded denims,
　　musty silks,
　　　　and faded memories
of princes
　　turned
　　　　to toads.

6

Beginning Again

Now I Want the Have

I've faced it then,
   have I?
      I suppose I have.
The magical
   answer
      to the cannonball
         question
"what do you
   really
      want?"
I have want,
   now I want
      the have,
the touch,
   the hand,
      the real,
the feel
   of the same
      leg
cast easily

over mine
   for a decade
      of winter
            mornings...
for two decades...
   or three...
that same leg
   flung
      over
         me,
the same smile.
   A sameness.
Oh, God, yes,
   I'd love that.
I've tasted
   the hors
      d'oeuvres,
nibbled
   at the cakes,
      the pies,
tasted
   all the lies
      of liberty
         and free.
Who sold me
   that?

I want mine
back,
the savage sweet
of same
and same
and same again
the same sweet man
to share
a life
of love
and have and same
with me.

Matador

I play
   a matador's game
     with life,
face it
   squarely,
     deceive
       its sharp
         horns,
wave
   embroidered
     glitter
       in its face,
I flaunt
   who
     I am,
and proudly,
   in the noonday
     sun,
I dance
   for no
     audience,
save
   my own

soul,
I lust not
for blood,
merely
for life.
I stand
here
alone,
with the
cape
in my hand,
I flee
not
from battle,
I laugh
when
I can.
Ha! Toro!
See me here,
see me
now!
See me, Life!
I am
a Woman!
I am
no man's
wife.

Are You Still There?

Leafing through
   the pages of my address book.
Looking for you,
    your name
      scribbled
        somewhere,
stuffed
   in my back pocket
     lo those many years
       ago.
Groping
   for you
     in the attic
       of my memory,
never
   lost,
     but put away.
Strange time
   to call perhaps,
     your name
       and face

retrieved
    so late
        after time
            has tossed us
both
    from here
        to there.
But now
    I'm here
        again.
            Are you?
Seven numbers
    and a long
        thin
            ring
                ringing on.
You must be
    gone.
        And then your voice
            again.
Surprising
    in its nowness
        right here
            in my room,
as I wonder how
    you look
        these days,

after such a lot
of years
pressed between
the pages
of a frayed
red leather book.

Snow in Your Hair

Snow
in your
hair,
not age,
warmth
in your
heart,
not rage,
a smile
in your
eyes
just for me.
I lean
gently back
and you
are my tree.
Your heart
has been
farther
than mine,

You love
   your cognac,
      your cigars,
         your white wine.
There's no
   haste
      in your
         pace,
you
   no longer
      must
         race,
no more
   do you flee
      or break
         dates,
no need
   to rush
      past,
         dodging fates.
You give me
   the sun
      and the moon
         in your palm,
you need me,
   you love me,

you make me
feel calm.
You gave me
the woman
I wanted
to be,
you hold me
so gently
and let me
feel free,
we stand
close together
and smile
at our truth.
You gave me
the sun,
now I give you
my youth.

Pretend
Forever

Devastating,
  debonair,
    delightful
      man,
and I,
  the dazzling
    darling,
as face to face
  we dance,
    we waltz,
we do a minuet
  of hope
    on our desert isle,
I laugh,
  you smile,
    we float
      with glee.
Together
  hand in hand,
    so free,
then suddenly

I see
   the narrow
      band
of gold
   that holds
      you fast,
         and at last
you see
   that I am
      fettered
         by the same,
and now
   it is
      a kind of game,
         as you hold
            my arm,
I touch
   your sleeve,
      enjoying
         the pretend
            forever
magic
   of our
      cinderella
         eve.

For a Year, For a Day

Music and singing
and laughter
and bringing
daffodils
to toss
in the air
and nary
a care,
and a river
to wear
and a sky
to put on
like
a cloak,
and Coke
to drink
and then
champagne

and carriage
    rides
        at midnight
            in the park,
and all
    a lark
        until
the gingerbread
    begins
        to crumble,
and at last
    you stand there,
        broken,
            foolish,
                humble.
Go ahead,
    sing.
        Don't wait
            for a ring.
Laugh
    while you may,
        for a year,
            for a day,
smile,
    and never look
        harried,

if the man
   you insist
      that you
         love
is
   already
      married.

Peacocks
and Frogs

Peacocks
   and frogs.
Princes
   and pickles.
Gingham
   and mustard
     and giggles
      and tickles.
Onions
   and daisies
and raindrops
   and stars.
Cheap wine
   and fine wine
    and love
     sold in jars.

Front page,
  back page,
    sports page
and financial
  section
    all a jumble?...
Oh, no,
  it is
    not I
      who'll make
        you mumble
in despair,
  wondering
    precisely
      where
the page one
  news
    has fled,
as you
  lie
    cozily
      abed,

sipping tea
     and smoking
while
     exasperatedly
          and in secret
               choking
wondering
     where
          in hell
               the Dow Jones
                    might be...
Oh, no...
     no sacred
          rite
to be
     defiled
          by me.
Separate
     papers,
          separate
               baths,
united joys
     delighted
          laughs,
the meeting
     of two

very
   independent
      sorts,
while above us
   one big
      bright star
         cavorts
and tall trees
   which gently
      flow and bend,
and in our laps,
   two morning
      papers,
sacred
   till the
      very
         end.

Too Much

Silence today...
  too busy?
    You couldn't
      get through?
What does it mean?
  Are you already bored?
    Does it matter?
      Is the telephone
        out of order?
I check my watch
  again
    and fiddle with
      the border
        on the bed,
running reasons
  through my head,
    thinking
      of all the possibilities,
why perhaps you
  couldn't call
    last night...

but still
    a chill
        of fright....
            Does it matter?
            Has he fled?
And slowly,
    I go back
        to bed,
heavy hearted,
    lonely,
        and a little bit afraid...
Have I played it wrong
    this time?
Too open?
    Too much too soon?
        Or is it something
            that I've said?
Or have I quickly become
    just anyone,
a someone to take
    for granted,
        an old shoe?
Or is it that I am
    already
        much too much
            in love
                with you?

Open Hand

Oh, such an open hand
  I hold out to you,
    so wide open,
      filled with my heart,
my soul,
  my life,
    my sins
      and pleasures
        and despairs.
It used to be
  that I held it all
    hidden
deep inside
  my pockets,
    for none to see,
no one to hurt
  or touch
    or tell,
yet already I know you
  so well,
    trust you so much,
that I hold it all
  out for you to touch

and see...
knowing that
you won't
hurt me,
oh, treasured,
gentle,
much loved man
to whom I hold out
my open hand.

Only Close

Yes, love,
  I know,
    it's hard
      for both of us...
my wanting,
  needing,
    hoping,
      waiting,
almost
  seeming
    to be baiting
as I reach
  out
    in a way
that fills
  you
    with
      fear...
it's
  all right,
    runner man,
it's okay,

yes
    I know
you'll stay
    while
        you can
then you'll
    go
and I'll
    grow,
and I'll
    cry
        for a while...
            ssshhh...
it's all right,
    darling,
        smile.
I shan't
    get you
        lost
            in a life
                that you dread.
as visions
    of wedding rings
        dance
            in your head.
Fear not,
    don't flee.

I only
want you
close
to me.

Fondly

I care about you.
   I like you.
I relate to you.
   I understand you.
I feel for you.
   I'm fond of you.
     You're dear.
Oh, no, my dear.
   You're not even
     here,
nor barely
   there
     with your "fond"
      words
that relate
   to like
     and care.
      You are nowhere.
I need you,
   want you,
     love you.

That's what's
really there,
but do you
dare?

The Inside of Your Arm

You make love to me
  as though
    you wore
      the manual
        on the inside of your arm.
You touch,
  you feel,
    you reel,
you slide
  along the inside
    of my thigh...
      you sigh,
you smile,
  you keep yourself aloof,
    you arch sharply
      toward the roof,
you moan,
  and then you glance
    to see if by chance

I am as transported
    as you want me
        to think you are...
but no,
    no different
        than the backseat of a car
        a century ago,
            and then as well
there's one tiny tender thing
    that you, m'friend,
        forgot
with all your ravishing,
    ravaging,
        macho, sexy, free!...
You never even kissed me.

Good-bye
  hello
    good-bye
      good-bye
hello.
  Hello
    once more.
      Yet again.
And then
  good-bye
    another
thousand
  times
    and
      more.
From
  the end
    to
      the beginning,
and then
  back
    again,

starting
   new,
      no longer
         starting
            fresh,
no
   fresh
      left.
And each
   hello
      has
         the echo
            of good-bye
hidden
   in
      its heart,
ah, yes,
   my friend,
      I know.
         Hello?
Yes.
   For a while.
      And then
         you too
            will
               go?

Twinkles and Sparkles

Twinkles
and sparkles
and horrible
shakes,
shivers
and giggles
and frivolous
quakes.
Vague looks
and dark looks,
odd thoughts
and green eyes.
Yesterday's
wonders.
Tomorrow's
good-byes?

First Hello

First hello
   on a bright
     spring day,
fresh green
   splashed
    on all
     the trees,
flowers
   everywhere,
    in my hair,
our hands,
   your voice,
a ferry boat
   ride,
    laughter,
     songs,
and ice cream
   cones
    on a newly
     painted
      bench.
Then summer
   was ours,

we held it
tight,
grew
brown
and strong
and gay,
sailing days,
and waterfalls,
and woods,
picnics
and promises
and time
always
wanting
to stand
still.
And after
all that,
autumn
came
as a surprise,
crept up,
unfurled
its golden
hair
and scarlet
wares,

it grew chilly,
     leaves fell
          as we began
               to drift,
we had
     no picnics
          left
               to share,
barely time
     it seemed
to remember
     spring
          and salute
               our first
                    hello
before
     we said
          our last
               good-bye.

Count

I used
   to count
      my men
but it
   embarrassed
      me,
well
   bred,
      well
         fed,
well
   led
      on a proper
         path
for one
   or two,
perhaps
   secretly
      a third,
         but not
            a fourth.

A fifth?
Good
God!
A sixth,
disgrace,
and the
seventh
could
only
make
me know
I was
a whore.
Now
I don't
count
my men
ever
any
more.

Friend

We compare notes,
  my friend and I...
    shyly, nervously,
      but strangely
willing to tell
  the truth
    about our youth,
      about our then,
        about our now....
How many have you had?
  Did you care
    about them all?
Were they young?
  old?
    splendid?
      tall?
You mean you had one too
  whose name
    you never did
      quite
        know?
All right, all right,
  I understand.

I had one too.
It made me grow.
And a man you clearly
didn't love,
the kind that made
you feel
a whore?...
I had one too...
yes.
What a bore...
and degrading.
It chewed a nibble
from my soul.
Oh, and one so old.
And two so young.
I've come unsprung.
I'm telling you all this?
about them all?
right up to the very end?
But you tell me too,
and I feel good,
loved, accepted,
understood,
sharing my victories
and disgraces,
tragedies
and comedies,

bruises and how they mend...
with one single, very special,
treasured
friend.

7

Love Lost
Once More

Sing Softly

Sing softly
   sadly
      hollow
songs
   of bygone
      days
and yearning
   dreams
      of once upon
        an almost time.
Sing gently,
   love,
      at eventide,
on wintry
   nights
      and summer
        days.
Sing to
   your other
      love,
        my love,
and if our time

should come
again,
come softly
to my door
by night.
You'll find me
waiting
for you
there.

Come Back

Funny
　　that they all
　　　　come back.
　　　　　　They always
　　　　　　do.
Back
　　they come
　　　　with a change
　　　　　　of heart,
long after
　　they had
　　　　gone.
Back
　　they come
　　　　with all
　　　　　　the words
　　　　　　　I wanted
once
　　to hear.
　　　　But they come
back
　　too late.

Ears
go deaf,
hearts
die,
moments
pass
and time
ceases
to be
of much
importance.
This time
make it
different.
Bring him
back
while I
still
care.

—*Broken Day*—

I bought
　　groceries,
　　　　forgot
　　　　　to wash
　　　　　　my hair,
picked up
　　a pack
　　　of cigarettes,
and
　　eighteen
　　　nails,
I had
　　a project,
　　　　forgot
　　　　　a lunch,
I think
　　it rained
　　　all
　　　　day,
all year,
　　all life
　　　gone
　　　　gray.

Someone
said
that
you
got
married
yesterday.

No Man, — Our Man

Was he a man
the man
who was
my man?
You know,
that man...
the man...
my man...
...her man.
The man
who was
her man,
was mine,
I thought,
and I hear
she thought
so too.
Foolish
to think
the man
was ours.

No man,
   our man,
      her man,
         my man,
and I only
   wonder
      now and then
         who is his
woman now?

Scoundrel Love

You ask me if I loved the man,
    unworthy as you say he was,
      it seems to me I did,
    my friend,
        without much reason,
          or a good "because."
What a wretch he is now,
    in my ever-clearing brain,
what a dandy, what a scoundrel,
    and, oh, my friend,
    how much pain
      he inflicted on my heart
        without ever looking back.
O alack!
    Plague take the rogue
    and curse his soul,
      what a devil was that man,
      what an evil sort of troll!
But was he really all those things?

Was he quite as vile as that?
Then why is it that I love him,
   sitting here
     and looking back?

He Calls

And now,
  at last,
    he calls,
in tears,
  in fears,
    in dread,
instead
  of having
    loved me
      then.
He calls me
  now,
  in pain,
    in grief,
      in guilt,
with endless sorrow
  for the old cruelties
    he once enjoyed
      so much.
I remember...
  and now
    I answer him
      with caution,

with a sigh...
a distant
something
in my eye,
not quite a tear,
no longer love,
almost anger,
yet
not
quite
hate,
too late...
he asks
if I will see him
and I answer,
cowardly,
vague,
muttering
"don't think I can"
to this
pitiful,
not quite,
too late,
guilty
man.

Octopus
Hectopus

Octopus
   Hectopus
      Hexagon
         Round
            Lovers
who cheat
   make their own
      wailing sound,
shrieking
   like banshees
      explaining their ways,
breaking
   all hearts
      till the end
         of their days.

Someday

Someday
  is a place,
    a time,
      a dream,
a blade of summer
  grass,
    dried out,
and reminiscent
  of a day
    when someday
was reality
  and filled
    with hope.
Someday
  was a word
    we used
      to taunt
        each other,
a distant spot
  we hungered for,
    but were anxious
      not to find
        too soon.

Someday
was a yearning,
a man I knew
and loved,
in a someday
sort of way,
because today
was never quite
his style.
Someday
was a child
we would have
had,
but didn't,
a time I knew
would come,
but never has.

To Clo:
Christmas
Remembered

The Christmas most dear to me?
    The one we danced beside the
    tree,
    The Christmas you lay next
    to me.
The year we shared each other's
hearts,
    The Christmas we were one.
Ah, dancing man of long ago,
    Come back to me again,
The tree is lit, my stocking's hung,
    I wait now as I have since then,
For but one more Christmas Eve,
    In the brilliance of our midnight
    sun.

Father,
Daughter,
Friend

Extraordinary moments
   stand out now,
special days,
   the big events,
     the times I can't forget...
my wedding day,
   riding in the car
     bathed in a cloud
      of white,
hidden by my veil,
   my hand clutched in yours,
and then you suddenly
   so pale
    as we walked
     up
      the aisle...
and then I smile,
   another time, another day,

while still a child,
wearing something ghastly,
　　wild,
and you pretending that
　　I looked okay,
　　　　beautiful, in fact,
　　　　　　divine...
do you remember
　　that funny time?
And then the times
　　you came to camp,
the day I broke your
　　favorite lamp,
the bookcase
　　I destroyed,
the absurdity of meeting
　　boys,
　　　　and bringing them to you...
the memories a kind
　　of glue
　　　　between my then
　　　　　　and now,
I see you with a furrowed brow
　　poring over
　　　　what I wrote,
scribbling, writing,
　　making notes,

and in later years,
only your voice
in the midnight hours,
as silently I dialed,
so relieved to find you there,
so good to know you cared,
how much we said,
how rich the gifts,
how lucky we both were
to have been father,
daughter, friend...
and even now, that you are
gone,
the joy of that will never end.

Crying Rainbows

Crying rainbows,
 dripping tears,
  reminding me
   of what you were
    to them,
I listen to your friends,
 I read the notes,
  I nod my head,
   I hold my pen,
I try to say
 the things
  they need
   to hear....
But what of me?
 Where will you be
  next week
   when I'm alone,
or when I want to send
 my book,
  who will look

at my work
the way you did?
Who will speak
the truth,
who will remind me
of my youth?
Must I be a grown-up
now
that you have fled?
Who will tuck me
into bed
if I wish to be
a child again
of one
or two
or three?
Who will take
care
of me
as you used to do?
Oh, Daddy, is it
true
that you are gone,
and I am grown?...
Yes, you are,
I am,

as I sit here,
all alone,
crying rainbows
of my own.

8

*And then
you
love again . . .
carefully
this time.*

Hurray for the Legalized Lover

Were they so wrong
     the madwomen
          of the fifties
who endowed
     each lover
          with the gift
               of wedlock?
Are we so much
     better off
          with bedlock?
Am I so free
     because
          I wear no ring,
and carry only
     my brave name
          after all
               these scars?

Ah, no,
   really,
      I think by now
I ought to
   have a medal
      or two,
a name or three
   or four
      or five.
After all
   is said
      and done
who will know
   that in fact
I was once
   very much
      in love, alive?
And with all
   our lively
      seventies games,
I begin
   to yearn
      for an endless
         fifties
            list of names.

If we're so free
   why should
      we be
         so very undercover?
Next time
   I think
      I'll find me
a name-throwing
   legalized
      lover.

Champagne
in My Shoe

Sitting here,
  with early
    morning coffee,
wondering
  where you are
    right now,
I still feel good,
  like well-polished wood,
well-oiled springs,
  waiting to see
    if the morning
      brings
you back,
  or will you wait
    till noon?
      So soon?
Or not until...
  tonight...
    and then a shaft
      of fright...

like sunbeams
   at my feet...
so sweet
   our hours
      before the dawn,
the dreams
   they spawned,
     the pains
      they stilled,
the tears they dried
   from years ago,
     oh, let it grow
all this bright
   new love
     I need so much,
your gentle touch
   like champagne
     in my shoe...
oh, dear new man,
   come back,
     come back,
I promise I'll be
   good
     to you....

Attic

Over the years,
  I have carried
boxes,
  treasures,
    objects,
      beds,
old shreds
  of people
    who had hurt
      or cared,
people I had pared
  down
    in memories
      and dreams,
people who had shrunk
  and grown,
    those who had left me
      all alone,
I carried them along,
  I sang their song,
  I kept their faces
    in sacred places
      in my mind,

a kind of album of my life,
my years as child,
my days as wife,
my broken toys,
my shattered joys,
lying in a myriad pieces
near my feet,
swept into piles
with all the smiles
that faded all too soon,
as I sat,
woven into the cocoon
you quietly unwound,
where somewhere
deep within
you found me
hidden,
playing with a doll,
a bear,
how much I care,
how good you've been
as I notice
what I should have seen
an eternity before...
the debris beneath the bed,
the brittle chaos in my head,
the wilted flowers,

forgotten hours,
the whispers and the taste
of ash
buried in the attic
of my not so many years,
and suddenly the tears
seem to have mattered not at all,
it is no longer fall
but spring
as you bring
me all this joy
to have and hold
and keep,
and I,
laughing,
pull aside the blinds,
let in the sun,
hitch up my skirts,
pick up the broom,
and finally,
begin
to sweep.

Brand-new
Now

Let us not
  confuse
    the actors
      in the play.
He hurt me,
  she broke
    your heart.
He left me,
  and she was
    a rotten cheat.
Let us instead
  see only
    each other.
You took
  my pencil,
I failed
  to wash
    the tub out,
      dry your razor,
we forgot
  to buy

a loaf of bread
for lunch.
Those are
our only
griefs
to cry for.
So if he
left me
long before
you came along,
I bid him now
adieu,
and if she left
you broken,
I'll help you
to begin anew.
And tomorrow
you'll give
back
my pencil,
I'll dry
your razor,
wash the tub out,
and we will buy
the bread
together,

and start
a solid
you-me-now
life.
Only me
and you.

Loving You

Childlike,
   I hear
      the echoes
         in the halls,
the footfalls
   that never came,
I hear the silence
   in the night,
I taste
   the fright,
and yet,
   I am a grown-up
      now,
         or so they say,
a mesh of gray
   woven into my hair,
      too old to care
         if the footsteps
            ever come again...
and yet,
   last night,
      I felt my heart

listen,
   tremble,
      wait,
fearful
   that I shan't find
      you
         waiting at the gate,
fearful that you'll
   cross
      the fields
         and vanish in the night...
too old
   for this fright,
it should not matter
   quite so much...
and yet
   it does...
      it does...
         you do....
The world
   would be
      my tomb
         again
were it not
   for the joy
      of loving you.

Matching the Pairs

The roof
  brought down
   around
    our ears,
the curtains
  wrapped
   around our
    heads,
all our apples
  so carefully
   stacked,
so instantly
  scattered,
   the patter
    of every day
halted
  as we sat there
suddenly
  lame,
suddenly tamed
  by life

and anger,
fear,
and despair,
dismay,
as we glared
from
opposite
corners,
throwing rocks
tossing dreams
like used socks
somewhere
behind us
into a place
we would never
find
again,
and then scurrying
about,
clutching
our accusations
in our arms,
the charms of each
forgotten
until the magic
clock
began to chime

the hour...
not quite midnight
yet,
still time,
a moment or two,
in which to run
and dash and hurry,
scurry about
again,
finding the socks,
washing them clean,
asking each other
"what did you mean,"
matching the pairs,
saying "I care,"
and just enough
time
to run
from doom,
and meet once again,
in the heart
of the room,
holding out hope,
baring our souls,
feeling my insides
no longer cold,
but slowly warm,

slowly glad,
slowly good,
slowly new,
and you with that
smile,
the same
much loved
you.

Morning
Friends

Quickly
    I pitter-pattered
        up the stairs,
knowing what I'd see
    as I juggled
        your usual breakfast
            order,
more or less,
    but never did I
        guess
that the scene
    I'd meet
would warm my soul
    and mist my eyes,
        and make me realize
            again
how much I care,
    how good you are,
        how sweet the scene
            I saw,

as I heard her whisper
  gently
    "please,"
seeing my daughter,
  her best doll,
    and her teddy bear
perched
  on your knees,
your sleepy face
  peeking between
    the mob
thronging
  in your arms
    as she held your hand
      and you his paw...
how much I loved
  all that
    I saw.

Joy

Joy
    in the morning,
        in our
dawn,
    in your
        sun,
joy
    in the morning,
being
    two,
        feeling
            one.
Your head
    on my pillow,
        my heart
            in your
                hand.
new life
    in our
        loving,
in our
    own
        magic
            land.

The Gift of Love

Ever hopeful,
    filled with dreams,
        bright new,
            brand-new,
                hopeful schemes,
pastel shades
    and Wedgwood skies,
        first light
            of loving
                in your eyes,
soon to dim
    and then you flee,
        leaving me
            alone
                with me,
the things I fear,
    the things you said
        burning rivers
            in my head,
bereft of all
    we shared,

my soul
  so old,
    so young,
      so bare,
afraid of you,
  of me,
    of life,
      of men...
until
  the bright new
    dreams
      begin again.
The landscape never
  quite the same,
    eventually
      a different game,
aware at last
  of what I know,
    and think,
    and am,
      and feel,
the gift of love
  at
    long
      last
        real.

9

...and then love is born again.

Tomorrow's Child

Small and warm,
tiny hands reach up
to touch and prod,
small toes stretch
and something deep inside
feels like the ripple
of a giggle,
as our tiny
precious
unborn child
begins
to laugh
and dance
and wiggle.

Moonbeam

How proud I am
　of all you are
　　and all you do,
how rich I feel
　when meshed
　　with you,
how strong
　I know
　　our love to be,
how lovely
　to be us,
　　yet free,
and how delicious
　this new gift,
　　this moonbeam
　　　in my soul,
this gift of you,
　this part of me,
how very loved
　our child
　　will be.

Come Soon

Waiting for you,
   little one,
      getting ready
a steady
   flow
     of rainbows
dancing through
   my head,
     the single thread,
       the constant theme,
       the tender dream
of you
   in our midst
     at last,
the planning
   and the hope,
     the gingham
and the little boat
   we bought you
     at a fair...
       ...oh, yes, we care...

we dream,
   we scheme,
     we wait,
we've found the house,
   the home,
     the room...
now, hurry, child,
   come to these
     waiting arms,
who long for you,
   come home,
     come now,
       come soon....

New Life

Silently, I watch you grow,
magically planted inside of me...
But soon I'll set you free,
sweet soul.
You are so small,
so big, so young, so old...
you push so hard
as though to shove me aside...
and soon my heart
will open wide
as the magic of your new life
is unfurled.
And you push yourself
into your world.
Go ahead, little one,
I wait here, to cheer you on....

Arrived!

You have arrived
  and safely,
    long awaited miracle,
precious bundle
  lying in my arms,
your eyes staring
  into mine
    as though asking
what took <u>me</u> so long
  to get here,
and I, laughing
  and crying all at once,
    hold you tighter,
      press you near,
feeling you
  so infinitely dear,
    so mine, so ours,
      sweet gift of joy...
the prince!
  The heir!
    Our baby boy!

The Joy of You

Yes, she was lovely too,
   your sister...
      she came with tissue paper
translucence,
   all white and pink
      and frail,
like porcelain lit from
   within,
      a child to dress in silks
         and pink ribbons,
so perfect,
   and delicate
      in her beauty...
while you, robust fellow,
   lie here,
      beautiful and rosy cheeked,
bright eyed,
   and looking as though
      you should be
         in a swing,

or chasing puppies,
    counting guppies,
or picking flowers in a field,
    eating candied apples,
or cookies,
    dripping crumbs,
        not sucking on my thumb,
as I eye you once again,
    wondering who you are,
        will be,
if you are like her
    or him
        or me,
if your eyes will be
    brown
        or blue,
and then I laugh again,
    overwhelmed
        by the sheer joy
           of you

Welcome Home

I have waited a lifetime for this,
   climbed mountains,
     counted dreams,
schemed and prayed
   and danced
     and would have,
       if I'd had to,
         drunk witches' brew...
I would have done all that,
   beloved babe...
     and more...
       just to have you...
I have waited,
   I have pined,
     sometimes cried,
       and never whined,
in silence and in darkness
   I have often prayed,
I have tried to forget the hoping,
   yet never ceasing to muse
     about this day...
wondering if...

wishing that...
        aching, longing,
and then finally knowing,
    growing,
        glowing,
overwhelmed with joy
    and gratitude...
and now this moment,
    you are here...
you've come at last,
    after waiting all these years...
        second child of my heart,
            sweet babe of my dreams,
holding fast to one finger,
    your eyes locked in mine,
your heart already sewn to my own...
    welcome, my darling...
        welcome at last,
            welcome, sweet babe...
Welcome home.

10

Love

Life with its odd endings
and beginnings,
its occasionally
very painful
middles,
its riddles,
its surprise hellos,
and at times
astonishing
adieus,
its greens, its grays,
its reds, its blues,
its flowers which come
like sunbursts
on a gloomy day,
given by a man
you barely know,
and its birthdays
forgotten
by the men
you love...
Life, with its rare gifts,

its strange charm,
its strong arm,
its vast sass,
its more than occasional
boot in the ass,
its blunt pain,
its bleak rain,
its sorrow
and its grief...
is somehow all too brief,
like a cinderella ball,
so deck the halls,
put on your pumps,
your furs,
your minks,
don't shrink,
put your tiara on,
step out,
prance high,
chin up,
dance nigh
the flame
with eyes aglow,
and above all, dear friends,
before you go,
before it ends,
and there remains

no further tale to tell,
dare once...twice...
often if you choose,
but dare,
yes, dare to love,
and if you do,
make sure that you
love well.
For love is worth it all,
is worth a call,
a dream,
a scheme,
a sleepless night,
a carriage ride,
or crossing
half the world,
for a glimpse, a touch,
a truth...
for love is youth,
is fun,
is grand...
a carnival...
an opera ball....
For truth to tell,
Love is Life...
and Life is Love...
and Love is All.